Deeper Mysteries
of the
SOUL

(Updated Edition)

Ebenezer & Abigail
Gabriels

Ebenezer & Abigail Gabriels
19644 Club House Road Suite 815
Gaithersburg, Maryland 20886
www.EbenezerGabriels.Org
hello@ebenezergabriels.org

DEDICATION

To Yahweh, To Elohim, To Adonai and to the Son of the Most
High God.
You are the Lover of our souls and the Purchaser of our souls.
Thank you for paying the costly price and redeeming our soul
with your powerful and precious blood back to the Lord.

CONTENT

1 Redeemed Soul   Pg 7

2 Soul   Pg 13

3 Body   Pg 20

4 Spirit   Pg 27

5 Mind   Pg 36

6 Dreams & Revelation   Pg 44

7 War against the Soul   Pg 48

8 Healed Soul   Pg 58

1

~

REDEEMED

SOUL

All souls belong to God. Some souls have been hijacked by the devil, and the goal is to lead those souls to hell. I was at a retail store in 2019. As I was waiting in the queue for my turn, I observed a mother shopping alongside her young son. She was about to make a payment for her purchase when the son insisted on getting a toy. Looking at the price tag, the mother realized she could not afford the toy, and the store attendant seemed to have caught what was happening. He quickly stepped in and said to the boy, "we do not have any type of this toy in stock anymore. We have ordered more and your mommy will buy for you in a few days when new supplies arrive at our store". The boy did not seem to be convinced, but the store attendant insisted. The mother joined the attendant in convincing the boy. And the boy reluctantly nodded, and he left the store with his mother. Then it was my turn to be attended to. I asked the store attendant, "are you serious that the toys are no longer in stock?". He said, "No, we have them". Then I asked him why he lied to the boy. He said, "I cannot allow him to be crying and making noise here when his mother cannot afford to buy him the toy". I asked him if he was a Christian. He said yes. I asked him what would happen to his soul if Jesus came right now. He didn't seem concerned about that. Like this young man, sin is part of the daily living of many, and yet, there is a great danger to the soul living in sin.

No Sin is Above God's Forgiveness: Not too Bad to Be Saved

There was a lady to whom we ministered. The Lord said to her that He wants to make her life beautiful, but she needs to turn away from her wicked ways and come to ask the Lord for mercy. I asked the Lord what that means, the Lord said, "She is not who she says she is". This lady was working in deep witchcraft, but she disguises herself as a Minister of God in their church. Immediately she realized that the Lord had revealed what she was doing, she fled and stopped coming to worship gatherings. There are many people like this lady who think they are too lost to be found by God. Many looks at the evil works they have done, and blatantly say "No" to salvation and continue in their old ways.

Some people have walked into unimaginable abominations. Some have prostituted themselves, some are living in adultery, and fornication, while others are enchanting - hiring satanic prophets for satanic assignments. While the Lord frowns at this, He is ready and eager to clean His people of all sins, and give them a new life. Unfortunately, many perceive themselves as "too lost to be saved", hence, hell becomes their eternal destination because of the rejection of the saving grace of our Lord Jesus.

Meeting The Real Jesus: A Lover and a Forgiver

This is why you need to be awakened to fight for your soul while you still have the opportunity, by giving your life in totality to Jesus, so He can redeem your soul with His blood. There is no type or magnitude of sin that the blood of Jesus cannot write off. God is a loving God, and that is contrary to the picture of God that the devil has painted in the minds of many. Many see God as a God who gives strict rules and punishes sinners. Our God is a God of many attributes. He is a loving Father, compassionate, kind, generous in mercy and the God who wants the best for His people. This is why He sent His Only Son, Jesus Christ to the world, to bear the burden of all our sins so that we do not have to pay for it with our blood. With the blood of Jesus in effect, the magnitude of the sinner's offense no longer counts. If the sinner returns to the Lord in repentance with a broken heart and contrite heart, the Lord will embrace the sinner and give them a new life.

Don't Be Limited by Shame: Jesus Has Conquered Shame

Shame is a terrible spirit. It makes sinners hide their sins and shy away from repentance. The spirit of shame pushes people to lie to themselves at the point of deliverance and release of grace. Shame seeks to hinder people from breaking free from the cords of sin. The spirit of shame causes sinners to normalize sin. This is why

Jesus has taken away all shame, and whoever comes to Jesus will be accepted just the way they are. The book of Isaiah 53:4-5 noted, "Surely He has borne our griefs And carried our sorrows; Yet we esteemed Him stricken, Smitten by God, and afflicted. But He was wounded for our transgressions, He was bruised for our iniquities; The chastisement for our peace was upon Him, And by His stripes, we are healed".

Taking an Action to Save Your Soul: How to Give Your Life to Jesus

Giving your life to Jesus is a giant step to take to assure eternal life. More important than marital, parenting, financial, and career decisions, the decision of salvation is the single most vital decision you would ever make in life. When you give your life to Christ, a divine exchange occurs, and Jesus steps up to take up your place in wrath for all the sins you have committed, while you become cleansed. Next, you begin to learn about the new pathways of Jesus, His prescribed way of how to live a life in Him and you give Jesus the entirety of your mind, soul, and body. God becomes first in your mind and as Matthew 22:37 says, You love the Lord with all your heart, with all your soul, and with all your mind. In this realm of giving your life to Jesus will you find rest for your soul. Pray the following prayers to give your life to Jesus with your whole heart.

PRAYERS TO GIVE YOUR LIFE TO JESUS

1. Lord, have mercy on me, I believe that Jesus Christ is your only Son whom you sent to die for my sins.
2. Father, forgive me of all my sins, in the name of Jesus.
3. I repent of all known sins in the name of Jesus.
4. Father, take away all my burdens, in the name of Jesus.
5. Cleanse me with your blood Jesus .
6. Lord, baptize me with the Holy Spirit and Fire, in the name of Jesus.
7. Help me grow in your Word, and in the company of heaven-going believers, in the name of Jesus
8. I pray for the power not to return to my vomit, in the name of Jesus.
9. I dedicate my life to you, in the name of Jesus.
10. Thank you Lord, for a new life in you.

Welcome to the body of Jesus Christ. Now that you are a follower of Christ, you can no longer knowingly engage in sinful acts. You will also have to live by the word of God which is the Holy Bible, to learn the way of God, what He delights in and what His assignment for you here on earth is. The rest of the chapters in this book will provide an understanding of the body, soul and spirit, and show you practical lessons on how to shield your soul from the enemy, for the devil is a thief looking to steal back your soul from you for his use. Do not allow him.

JOURNAL

2

~

SOUL

The subject of the soul is one of the hard-to-explain mysteries that every heaven-going believer should seek to understand. As a new believer or a growing believer, it is important to study this subject because you have a soul which is the essence of life. The Lord has given us some revelation into the deep mystery of the soul and we share in the upcoming paragraphs and chapters.

The Scripture rightfully says in Hebrews 4:12:

" For the word of God is living and powerful, and
sharper than any two-edged sword, piercing even to the
division of soul and spirit, and of joints and marrow, and is a
discerner of the thoughts and intents of the heart"
Hebrews 4:12

This Scripture talks about the connections between the soul and the spirit, and also the advanced connection with the hearts which is the mind. Due to the closeness of the spirit, soul, and mind, only the Word of God has the accuracy and sharpness to slash through and divide to help us distinguish between these mysteries.

What is the Soul?

The soul is the formless essence of a man's existence. It is the seat of existence and the priciest portion of humans. It is the first element of man created before the other elements namely the body, spirit, and mind were created. In this section, we study the attributes of the soul.

In the creation of man, the soul is the first to be created. In Psalm 139, God reveals to David the mystery of the soul;

> For You formed my inward parts;
> You covered me in my mother's womb.
> I will praise You, for I am fearfully *and* wonderfully made;
> Marvelous are Your works, And *that* my soul knows very well.
> My frame was not hidden from You, When I was made in secret,
> *And* skillfully wrought in the lowest parts of the earth. Your eyes saw my substance, being yet unformed. And in Your book they all were written, The days fashioned for me,
> When *as yet there were* none of them.
> **Psalm 139:13-16**

Deeper Mysteries of the Soul

The Soul is the Intelligent Essence of Life: This Scripture reveals that the soul was created before the body was made. After the creation of the soul, the soul became aware of its existence and was amazed at the wonder of God's craftsmanship. The soul observed how God designed and fabricated the inner parts and the body of man before it was placed into the womb. The soul of man witnessed the creation of man's body. Hence, the body was designed to contain the soul, hence the body is only a vessel, while the soul is a major content of the human vessel.

The Soul is Accountable to All Deeds of Man: The soul is the entity in man that is held liable for all man's doing here on earth. In other words, the soul pays for every debt owed through sin and also gets all the blessings for every lifestyle that translates into righteousness. Despite its intangibility, it is the seat of life. This is why we define the soul as the formless entity of man that forms the basis of the mind and the center-point of the life of man.

The State of the Soul is Evaluable: The soul is highly evaluable. The only criterion for evaluating the soul is salvation. God evaluates the state of a soul by whether it is saved or not. In this case, salvation means whether the soul has been redeemed by the blood of Jesus or not. If the soul has been redeemed, it is saved and prospers otherwise it has been lost to the devil and dies.

The Price of the Soul: The cost of the soul cannot be estimated in numbers or in dollar value. The blood of Jesus was paid as a price to redeem every soul, this is why humans cannot be purchased. Due to the inestimable cost and expensiveness of the soul, God had to let go of the life of His only Son, Jesus, and accepted it as the only currency of worth for the redemption of the soul. For this reason, the soul is satan's greatest target.

The Soul the Nurturing Ground of all Emotions: The subject of the soul can be understood better when we take a look at where emotions originate from. The fruits of the Holy Spirit mentioned in the book of Galatians 5 namely love, joy, peace, patience, gentleness, self-control, kindness, and faithfulness - all originate from the soul. This is why it is important for the believer to have a firm understanding of the subject of the soul. A person who expresses love does so from the soul, and so is a person who is joyful. Also, conditions like anxiety originate from the soul. Every emotion expressed first originates from the soul.

PRAYERS TO SHIELD THE SOUL

1. My soul shall not be led astray in the name of Jesus.
2. My soul shall not be traded in the name of Jesus
3. My soul is shielded with the fire of the Holy Spirit.
4. My soul shall not be bewitched in the name of Jesus.
5. My soul shall not harken to satanic summoning in the name of Jesus.
6. Satanic intrusion is not granted into my soul in the name of Jesus.
7. The Lord Jesus is the keeper of my soul, in the name of Jesus
8. My soul rejects demonic summoning in the name of Jesus
9. My soul shall not be summoned into demonic courts, in the name of Jesus
10. All satanic gatherings of demonic elders making enchantments to lure my soul to demonic courts is scattered in the name of Jesus
11. All types of satanic arrows targeted at my soul shall return back to its senders in the name of Jesus
12. My soul, magnify the Lord with songs of worship, in Jesus name
13. My soul rejects oppression in the name of Jesus
14. My soul rejects suppression and depression the name of Jesus
15. My soul has been redeemed by the blood of Jesus
16. My soul belongs to the Lord Jesus.

17. The Lord shall protect His interests and investments over my soul in the name of Jesus

JOURNAL

3

~

BODY

The body of man is the container of the soul. Also called the flesh, in this chapter, we use flesh and body interchangeably. The flesh makes up a major part of our physical appearance. Moses received revelations from God concerning some of the secrets to the creation of Adam as seen in Genesis 2:7 :

And the LORD God formed man *of* the dust of the ground
Genesis 2:7a

What is the Body?

The body is the tangible structure containing the soul, the mind and the spirit of man. The Scripture revealed that God made the body of man from the dust of the ground. When Adam was cursed because of his iniquity in Eden, the Lord openly declared that man was made from dust and will return to being dust. In other words, God told Adam, this is the material used in creating your body, and your body will eventually return to being that material.

> In the sweat of your face you shall eat bread
> Till you return to the ground,
> For out of it you were taken;
> For dust you *are,*
> And to dust you shall return."
> **Genesis 3:19 (NKJV)**

The Body is the Container of the Soul: As we discussed in the first chapter, the soul needed a body and a spirit to become a living being. The Scriptures explain what happened in the creation of Eve in Genesis 2:21-22:

> "And the Lord God caused a deep sleep to fall on Adam, and he slept; and He took one of his ribs, and closed up the flesh in its place. Then the rib which the Lord God had taken from man He made into a woman, and He brought her to the man"
> **Genesis 2:21-22 (NKJV)**

The last sentence in the Scripture quoted above notes, Then the rib which the Lord God had taken from man He made into a woman - telling us what went into the creation process, and the next words say and He brought her to the man - this second statement indicates that the woman was taken away at some point from Adam during the creation process before she was brought back to Adam. Another Scripture tells us where Eve was taken. We find that Scripture in Psalm 139: 15-16.

> My frame was not hidden from You,
> When I was made in secret,
> *And* skillfully wrought in the lowest parts of the earth.
> Your eyes saw my substance, being yet unformed.
> And in Your book they all were written,
> The days fashioned for me,
> When *as yet there were* none of them."
> **Psalm 139: 15-16 (NKJV)**

The Body was Created to House the Soul: This Scripture explains that the creation of the soul was done in private. Though Adam's rib was a major component of Eve's body, God still took Eve into His secret place to create a body for her. This tells us that every soul had one-on-one time with God at the moment of creation. Also, this reveals that no other person is invited when a soul undergoes the creation process; only God is present. The soul of man is designed and created in the place of utmost security with a great deal of privacy. And the body is made, as a house for the soul.

The Body is the Gatekeeper to the Soul: The body is quite influential because it is the frontline of the mind and soul and has access points into the soul. Major access points into the soul include the eyes, the skin, the ears, the mouth, and the reproductive organs. Examples include - When your eyes are exposed to pornography materials, this alters the thoughts, and re-directs the desires of the heart, thereby brings pollution to the soul. Other examples: hearing certain types of stories may trigger reactions or weigh down on the countenance of the soul, eating the wrong type of food at the wrong time may wear out the soul, unholy sexual intercourse causes pollution to the soul.

The Body Houses God's Spirit and Presence: As a container, the body carries the Spirit and the presence of God, and is a temple to God. The body can carry the power of God such that when a person gets to a place, healing powers are released into a place. In the other way, the body can also carry several demons and can be used as the habitation of satan. This occurred in the ministry of Jesus as found in the book of Luke.

"Now in the synagogue there was a man who had a spirit of an unclean demon. And he cried out with a loud voice, saying, "Let *us* alone! What have we to do with You, Jesus of Nazareth? Did You come to destroy us? I know who You are—the Holy One of God!"But Jesus rebuked him, saying, "Be quiet, and come out of him!" And when the demon had thrown him in *their* midst, it came out of him and did not hurt him."
Luke 4:33-35 (NKJV)

The spirit of God can inhabit a body. Evil spirits can also inhibit a body. The body is by far, the most vulnerable out of the basic elements.

PRAYERS TO SUBJECT THE BODY TO THE POWER OF GOD

1. My body belongs to the Lord Jesus in the name of Jesus

2. My body shall not become a snare to my soul in the name of Jesus

3. My body is the temple of the Holy Spirit in the name of Jesus.

4. My body is placed under the subjection of the Holy Spirit in the name of Jesus.

5. My body shall yield to the word of God in the name of Jesus

6. My body shall not push me into hell in the name of Jesus

7. The blood of Jesus shall be the protection over my body, spirit, mind and soul in the name of Jesus.

8. The body shall not give the wrong access to my soul, mind and spirit in the name of Jesus

9. My body shall host God's presence in the name of Jesus

10. My body is dedicated to the Lord Jesus, in the name of Jesus.

JOURNAL

4

~

SPIRIT

Life comes from God. The book of John 1:4 notes, "In Him was life, and life was the light of men". This means that God owns life, and only Him supplies life. The Scripture describes how humans receive life from God and we explain that in this chapter.

The Sequence of Creation

The sequence of creation is the order to which the elements that make up the living being are created as described in the Holy Scriptures. Apostle Paul said in 1 Corinthians 15:46 "However, the spiritual is not first, but the natural, and afterwards the spiritual".

The sequence of creation is as follows:

> **Order 1:** The soul is created first. This is found in the book of Psalm 139:16 where David stated "your eyes saw my substance being yet unformed. And in your book they all were written, the days fashioned for me when as yet there were none of them"
>
> **Order 2:** Next is the body. This is found in the book of Genesis where the account of what God told Adam was captured in Genesis 3:19 - "... For dust you are, And to dust, you shall return."
>
> **Order 3:** And then the Spirit of Life is released for the completion of God's works in man as found in the Scripture below, Genesis 2:7

The Scripture quoted below shows that the soul and body still needed a spirit before a living being is formed. This means every person alive has a spirit. This spirit represents the spirit of God responsible for giving life. It is called the *Spirit of Life*. The Spirit of Life is given through the breath of God.

> "And the Lord God formed man *of* the dust of the ground, and breathed into his nostrils the breath of life; and man became a living being."
> **Genesis 2:7 (NKJV)**

The Spirit of Life connects humans to the abundance of God's life. The purpose of this connection is to allow life to flow from God to man during his timeline on earth. More revelations into the subject of the Spirit of Life are found in the book of Psalm 104, verses 29 and 30. This first verse explains that death occurs when God's breath which supplies the Spirit of Life is withdrawn. The second explains that during creation, the Spirit of Life is sent forth, and this is when a man receives the first breath and becomes a living being.

" You hide Your face, they are troubled;
You take away their breath, they die and return to their dust.
You send forth Your Spirit, they are created;
And You renew the face of the earth".
Psalm 104: 29-30 (NKJV)

Jesus Explains the Spirit of Life

Jesus's last word further explains the relationship between the Spirit of Life and the breath that we breathe in the Scripture quoted below:

"And when Jesus had cried out with a loud voice, He said, "Father, 'into Your hands I commit My spirit.' " Having said this, He breathed His last.".
Luke 23:46 (NKJV)

The verse above explains that when Jesus was about to depart the world, He handed over His spirit back to God, and ceased breathing.

Stephen's Revelation of Jesus as the Author of Life

We see a similar revelation in the life of Stephen when he was being stoned.

> As they stoned him, Stephen prayed, "Lord Jesus, receive my spirit."
> **Acts 7:9 (NKJV)**

The Scriptures noted a description of Jesus in the book of Acts 3:15 as the Author of life". This was what Stephen knew when he released his spirit back to the Lord Jesus as he approached the end of his time on earth.

Ezekiel's Revelation into the Spirit of God's life

God gives the perfect depiction of the spirit to Ezekiel. In the following Scripture:

> Then he said to me, "Prophesy to the breath; prophesy, son of man, and say to it, 'This is what the Sovereign Lord says: Come, breath, from the four winds and breathe into these slain, that they may live.'" So I prophesied as he commanded me, and breath entered them; they came to life and stood up on their feet—a vast army. Then he said to me: "Son of man, these bones are the people of Israel. They say, 'Our bones are dried up and our hope is gone; we are cut off.' Therefore prophesy and say to them: 'This is what the Sovereign Lord says: My people, I am going to open your graves and bring you up from them; I will bring you back to the land of Israel. Then you, my people, will know that I am the Lord, when I open

your graves and bring you up from them. I will put my Spirit
in you and you will live, and I will settle you in your own land.
Then you will know that I the Lord have spoken, and I have
done it, declares the Lord.'"

Ezekiel 37:9-14 (NKJV)

The above Scripture gives another explanation to the word
"breath". The word breath means the Spirit of Life supplied by
God through His breath, as verse 14 says," <u>I will put my Spirit in
you and you will live.</u>

The Dry Bones: Relationship Between the Body & the Spirit

We would understand the body and the spirit when we
draw examples from our mobile phones. The hardware is the
physical part that we touch and the mobile network is the spirit.
This is one of the easiest ways to look at it. The hardware of a
phone is like the body of a man while the network on a phone is
like the spirit in the body of a man. This explanation can be
applied to the dry bone that was shown to the prophet Ezekiel in
the following Scriptures.

He asked me, "Son of man, can these bones live? I said,
"Sovereign Lord, you alone know. Then he said to me,
"Prophesy to these bones and say to them, 'Dry bones, hear the
word of the Lord! This is what the Sovereign Lord says to
these bones: I will make breath enter you, and you will come to

life. I will attach tendons to you and make flesh come upon you and cover you with skin; I will put breath in you, and you will come to life. Then you will know that I am the Lord.'"

Ezekiel 37: 3-6 (NKJV)

The Sequence of Revival and Restoration

The sequence of revival is different from the one of creation as mentioned earlier in the chapter. and it goes as follows;

> **Order 1:** Breath is restored to supply life
> **Order 2:** Flesh is also restored

Studying the two sequences from the Scripture quoted above: The Scripture noted, <u>I'll make breath enter you, and you will become life</u>; without the breath, the bones cannot become life. <u>"I will attach tendons to you and make flesh come upon you and cover you skin,</u> this further reveals how God builds up the body of man. <u>I will make breath enter you, and you will come to life. I will attach tendons to you and make flesh come upon you and cover you with skin; I will put breath in you, and you will come to life.</u>

Observe that there is no third sequence mentioned above and in the Scriptures underlined: The soul is the only element that is not revived in the sequence of revival because the soul was not destroyed when the flesh was destroyed and the Spirit of Life withdrawn, the soul still existed. This is why restoration came after God restored His breath and flesh in the book of Ezekiel 37.

Other Functions of the Spirit of Life

The Gift of Life: The spirit of God given through the breath of God at the time of creation is available to all men for the purpose of life. Everyone, a believer in Jesus and non-believer has a portion of the breath of God in them, which is the spirit of God that supplies life.

As a Lamp to Search the Heart of Men: For the purpose of searching the heart of every human and taking account of the thoughts of men.

> The spirit of a man *is* the lamp of the Lord,
> Searching all the inner depths of his heart.
> **Proverbs 20:27 (NKJV)**

Lastly, it is worth noting that the Spirit of Life is different from the Holy Spirit which is released to everyone who believes Jesus is Lord and Savior. The Holy Spirit is a promise that is fulfilled at the time of salvation. The baptism of the Holy Spirit is needed to come upon believers to receive God's direct power, to overcome the world.

Those who do not have the knowledge of the Lord Jesus Christ as Savior do not receive the Holy Spirit, they only have the Spirit of Life for the purpose of living.

PRAYERS FOR THE SPIRIT

1. Father, let your life flow into my life, in the name of Jesus.
2. The supply of the breath of God shall not be cut off from me in the name of Jesus.
3. Father Lord, breathe upon me in the name of Jesus.
4. My spirit is strengthened by the fire of the Holy Spirit.
5. Lord Jesus, breathe the breath of life upon me in the name of Jesus.
6. Your breath shall not become stale in my life in the name of Jesus.
7. I shall worship the Lord with the breath that He has given me in the name of Jesus.
8. The breath of God in me shall not be polluted in the name of Jesus.
9. The devil shall not snatch the breath of God from me in the name of Jesus.
10. My spirit man is strengthened by the power of the Holy Spirit in the name of Jesus.

JOURNAL

5

~

MIND

In this chapter, the mind, the brain and the heart are used interchangeably. Taking lessons from computers. Computers need constant maintenance, and in the world's history, there's no computer yet that has run non-stop for 20 years without the need for a shut down for service. It is not so with the brain. Brain is developed right from the womb, and is designed by God to function.

What is the Mind?

In the brain is the dwelling place of the mind and the mind is the dwelling place of the soul. Spiritually, the combination of the soul and mind can be referred to as the "head". The mind is a shield to the soul, it is the central spot for all reasoning to fulfill our life's purposes. This is why the Scripture tells us to to place a guard around our minds;

More than anything you guard, protect your mind, for
life flows from it.
Proverbs 4:23 CSB

Function of the Mind and its Relationship with the Soul

The Mind is the Control Center of the Soul: The mind
shapes the direction of the soul. soul. As the mind of a person is,
so is their soul. Whatever is allowed into the mind defines the
state of the soul. The mind holds the key to the soul. Once the
mind of a person is secured, the soul is in safety. If the mind of a
person is exposed, the soul is unsafe and stands a risk of enemy
invasion. The soul is like a sponge absorbing anything the mind
feeds it. It is under the control of the mind, and highly
susceptible to the influence of the mind, whether good or bad.

The Mind Provides Food for the Soul

The soul needs nourishment, hence receives food from the mind.
The Scripture notes in Psalm 107:9 - "For He satisfies the longing
soul, And fills the hungry soul with goodness". This is why any
type of imagination that goes through the mind feeds the soul.
The mind is capable of feeding the soul from images, videos,
conversations and everything captured from the physical realm.
As a result, Scripture tells us to think of goodness and meditate
on it.

Finally, brethren, whatever things are true, whatever
things *are* noble, whatever things *are* just, whatever things *are*
pure, whatever things *are* lovely, whatever things *are* of good
report, if *there is* any virtue and if *there is* anything
praiseworthy—meditate on these things.
Philipian 4:8 (NKJV)

The Mind: Base of Faith
The mind forms the base of acceptance or rejection of salvation.
When a person hears the gospel, they make a decision in their
minds whether they accept Jesus as Lord and Savior or not. The
mind is where this decision takes place. If the mind says "no",
there is no entry for that soul into eternal life. As a result, the
mind is a prominent force that is capable of allowing salvation or
hindering salvation. For this reason, the Scripture noted, in
Romans 1:28 "And even as they did not like to retain God in
their knowledge, God gave them over to a debased mind, to do
those things which are not fitting". It is therefore vital to watch
over our minds to guard our faith.

Risk Facing the Mind of a Believer

Mind: A Target of the Enemy: To invade the soul of man, the
enemy targets the mind, using different tactics. One of the ways
to get into the soul of a person is through satanic content,
destructive doctrines in writings, explicit movies, magazines and
blog contents. The soul by itself cannot get access to these
materials but is processed through the mind. Once the brain

processes the experience after viewing satanic contents, it classifies the experience into good or bad based on what it feels after the experience. This good or bad experience goes into the soul and the soul feeds on it. The soul becomes reprogrammed to desire such images, and begins to demand to be fed by the mind with such polluted materials.

Another way the enemy tries to bypass the mind to get to the soul is through the use of drugs and substances. Here is why witchcraft is highly connected to drug and alcohol abuse. Witchcraft uses alcohol to get hold of people's reasoning to enter into their souls. Any drug that alters the state of the mind is highly detrimental to the soul of man.

The Mind's Power of Choice
God has given men the power of choice. The power of choice is a special type of power used by the mind to make decisions. The Scripture notes in the book of Deuteronomy 19:30

> I call heaven and earth as witnesses today against you,
> *that* I have set before you life and death, blessing and cursing;
> therefore choose life, that both you and your descendants may
> live;" .
> **Deuteronomy 30:19 (NKJV)**

God does not enforce His law upon us. He gives the power and freedom to make choices. Sometimes people use this power against God. As a result, the devil is constantly bringing confusion, and influencing decision making, to push people into making blatant choices against God's will. The forces of the enemy try to deceive and take over the mind during decision-making. A mind is a place of war. The enemy sometimes uses gentle persuasion and aggression which is also called excessive force.

Gentle Persuasion: The enemy whispers, "if you accept Jesus, what would people think of you? You have been practicing this religion for 50 years, in fact, your parents practiced this religion, and now you want to follow Jesus" Thoughts like this begin to rise up in the heart and seek to steal salvation

Aggression/Excessive force: To prevent people from salvation, the devil uses the tactic of scolding or threatening, saying, "If you become a Christian, I will divorce you, or I will disown you". It could be a husband telling the wife, or a parent telling a child. The enemy's goal is to cause fear.

When a person is considering whether to give their life to Jesus or not, the enemy seeks to lock their mind with his invisible chains, to keep their mind closed and hardened to the gospel. This is why those who go out to preach the gospel should begin with deep intercession for the mind of the hearers of the world to be open.

Managing and Controlling your Thoughts with the Word of God

What's on your mind? What are you thinking of? What are the thoughts that fill up your heart? All of the thoughts in your mind matter to God, because they are the food that your soul consumes. With the type of capabilities given to the mind, the mind is able to bring into reality the thoughts it conceives. This is why the word of God is the only weapon strong and powerful enough to nurture the thoughts formed in the mind.

> Therefore you shall lay up these words of mine in your heart and in your soul...
> **Deuteronomy 11:18a NKJV**

Meditation on the Word of God is the only way to keep our minds healthy and our souls guarded at all times. It shields the mind against all types of infiltration of the enemy and also stands as the strongest defense against all enemy fire against the mind.

PRAYERS FOR A SOUND MIND

1. My mind is the mind of the Lord Jesus Christ
2. My mind is protected by the fire of the Holy Spirit in the name of Jesus.
3. My mind shall not be hijacked by the devil in the name of Jesus.
4. My mind is not the laboratory of darkness in the name of Jesus.
5. My mind is connected to the mind of the Father in the name of Jesus.
6. My mind shall not conceive evil in the name of Jesus
7. My mind is purified by the Holy Spirit and fire in the name of Jesus.
8. My mind is renewed and transformed in the name of Jesus.
9. The Word of God fills up my mind in the name of Jesus.
10. My mind shall not be corrupted in the name of Jesus.
11. My soul is fed with the Word of God in the name of Jesus.
12. When I am about to make decisions of my destiny, let my mind yield only to the power of the Lord and the word of God in the name of Jesus.

JOURNAL

6

~

DREAMS & REVELATIONS

The process of how the soul and mind work on dreams is addressed in this chapter.

How Dreams are Processed: Soul and Mind

God reveals revelations through dreams to the soul. This information is then downloaded into the soul. The soul passes the information to the mind for playback and for translation. By itself, the soul cannot translate this information. The soul has no context for physical things and needs the Mind as an interpreter of information. It then says, "Mind, explain this to me". The Mind explains based on the development of the mind and the exposure of the mind to the knowledge of the Word of God and the knowledge of the outside world. When the soul gets the meaning of certain information, the soul reacts to that information either positively or negatively.

How the Enemy Interferes with the Soul of People

Some Satanists disguised as massage professionals endanger the souls of many telling people they have the ability to take away all their stressful emotions and transfer them unto themselves in the process of a massage. As discussed in earlier chapters, the human senses are some of the access points into the soul, and when people submit their bodies to the wrong individuals with satanic spirits for ungodly practices like yoga, mind, and palm-reading, the soul gets invaded and polluted is introduced. All these satanic practices are employed by those who have learned the satanic ways of assessing the soul. Here is why many believers no longer hear from God directly, because they have opened up their souls to filth and demonic deposits. Every information, dream, and vision given by God is released through the Holy Spirit to the soul, which then passes it to the mind for translation. A person whose soul is fed with the word of God and whose mind is watered with the word of God is in the best place to receive from God.

However, a person whose soul is fed with the affairs of the world, junks, gossip, malice, sex outside of marriage does not receive the downlooads from God, but from satan. Infact, many people who receive revelation receive from the devil, thinking they are receiving from God, when their streams are polluted. There are so many teachers, prophets, leaders today whose stream has been corrupted, and whose souls are being fed by demons.

PRAYERS FOR YOUR DREAM LIFE

1. My dream life shall receive the touch of God in the name of Jesus.
2. My mind receives the empowerment of the Holy Spirit in the name of Jesus.
3. My soul shall receive the power of the Holy Spirit in the name of Jesus.
4. My soul shall not be polluted in the name of Jesus.
5. All types of wrong signals sent to my soul are cast out in the name of Jesus.
6. Lord, let my soul receive upliftment from the Holy Spirit in the name of Jesus.
7. My soul shall not yield to the enemy in the name of Jesus.
8. I receive the power of God's accuracy in dream translation in the name of Jesus
9. Thou my soul, Jesus Christ is Lord over you.
10. My soul belongs to Jesus Christ.

JOURNAL

7

~

WARS

AGAINST THE

SOUL

Now that we've studied the soul, body, spirit and mind, let's revisit the question, "what is the soul"? Let's refresh on some of the revelations found on this subject.

The soul is formless and can be likened to a sponge which absorbs the content of the mind to take shape. The mind is the control center where the soul takes direction from. The soul cannot process information received from the Lord by itself, it is influenced by the mind. Let's learn from the example of the souls of young children whose minds are shielded from the contamination of the world. Parents sometimes hear children saying, "I want to become a doctor when I grow up. I want to become a fireman when I grow up". They speak about the revelation their souls have received. This is what has been implanted as their direction in life from God. If those purposes are not carefully nurtured, they lose the vision for it when the mind becomes corrupted as they grow. To guard against this, believers need to continue to have their mind dedicated to the Lord for an incorruptible direction into God's purposes through us on earth.

Spiritual Wars Against the Soul :A Soul at War
The war against the soul is one that originates from the flesh. The soul faces several attack risks from the flesh (the body) and the Scripture says in 1 Peter 2:11 "fleshly lust wars against the soul". If not overcome by the power of God, the flesh can become highly lethal against the soul. This is what happens when people become restless until they commit a sin and are chased out of God's presence. This is the workings of the flesh. This fleshly lust causes people not to stop until they enter into the strife of tongues, sexual immorality and all sorts of actions the Scripture warns against.

Spiritual Wars Against the Soul : Sickness of the Soul
A soul can get sick. Many souls are sick because they are in a defeated state and unable to get out of the captivity of sin. When the soul is sick, it is lost, and kicked out of God's presence. A sick soul is high-risk, because it's already in the hands of the enemy. It continues in sin and has normalized to a sinful life.

Lord, be merciful to me; heal my souls, for I have sinned
against you
Psalm 41:4 (NKJV)

Spiritual Wars Against the Soul: Soul Trading

Another type of war the soul fights is the war that the enemy
wages to steal a soul and begins transacting with the soul. There is
a hidden soul trade market in the dark places of the world where
the souls of men and women are bought and traded. There are
many soul hunters around believers, sent by Satan and seeking
ways to capture the soul of a believer for the devil. Soul trading
occurs when the enemy goes with an accusation before the court
of God and negotiates for a soul; giving God strong reasons why a
soul does not belong to the kingdom of God. The devil goes
frequently to negotiate for the souls of sinners to get his final
home (hell) crowded. The soul is susceptible to satan when there
are compromises found, and that compromise is sin. Once a soul
is found guilty of the enemy's accusation, the soul is handed over
to the enemy. Sin is the currency used by the devil to purchase
souls. Many souls have been traded already, and these souls have
no place in eternity to reign with the Lord Jesus. If there's any
active and known sin in your life, your soul is at risk. Sins like
fornication, adultery, lies, witchcraft, and unbelief are all reasons
why people are thrown into hell regardless of how good their
intentions were. The following Scripture reveals the realness of
soul-trading;

Our *soul* has escaped as a bird from the snare of the fowlers;
The snare is broken, and we have escaped.
Psalm 124:7 (NKJV)

God is all out at war against the traders of soul that He curses them. Christians must also be aware and radically guard their soul against the trading of their souls. There are people we encounter every day whether in corporate workplaces, schools, gatherings of worship, malls, or parking lots, pretending to be acquaintances, and well-wishers that are soul hunters working for satan. Many of them use charms to hunt souls. They lure with material things, money, food, and false friendship, just to harvest saved souls.

Therefore thus says the Lord God: "Behold, I *am* against your *magic* charms by which you hunt souls there like birds.
Ezekiel 13:20 NKJV

These are the most popular tactics for soul hunting: The enemy knows how to lure unsteady souls into the nest. God's children will do well by staying rooted in the Spirit of God.

Common Tactics for Soul Trading

Spiritual Wars Against the Soul: Soul Trading by Unholy Sexual Relations: The enemy uses different tactics for soul-trading. The fastest way the soul of a person is caught is through sexual relationships outside of marriage. Soul traders look for just one opportunity for sinful sexual encounters, because it is the fastest way to lose God's presence and protection. The soul traders do not hunt for common men, but constantly in search of men and women destined for God's great purposes. The Scripture warns in Proverbs 7:25 to 27, "Do not let your heart turn aside to her ways, Do not stray into her paths; For she has cast down many wounded, And all who were slain by her were strong *men,* Her house *is* the way to hell, Descending to the chambers of death". This is why the Scriptures warn His children to flee from all appearances of evil.

Spiritual Wars Against the Soul : Soul Trading by Exposure to Wrong Food

The stomach is also an input device to the soul. Overeating can weary the soul. Some foods are an abomination to the soul of a believer. Job talked about abominable food to his soul.

My soul refuses to touch them; they're as loathsome food to

me

Job 6:7

The intake of food is one of the ways the enemy can assess the souls of people, and this is why it is a huge risk for those who are unable to control their appetite. Anyone who eats anything without caution is highly prone to soul hunters, and such destinies are not secure. By food, Esau lost his birthright to Jacob. There are a lot of soul traders who are restaurant operators. Only the Holy Spirit of God can help a believer discern the right places to eat.

Spiritual Wars Against the Soul: Soul Trading by Satanic Music

Music has to do with sounds and is one of the fastest ways to connect to the soul. Music cuts through the body into the mind and the soul faster than any other means. This is why people can get inspiration through music. Music is played and all of a sudden, forgotten ideas are brought back to memory. Our body responds to rhythms by the music we hear. This is an area where the devil has studied and circulated satanic music to subscribe people's minds to the wrong doctrine, and demonic groups, and causes people to lose their minds. The lyrics of satanic music and its melodies are composed in covens, underwater, and in the dark places of the world to infest minds and souls with demons. The devil is able to legally claim ownership of those minds and souls because they willingly submitted to his music.

Spiritual Wars Against the Soul: The Tool of Words

Last, we discuss soul trading by words. Words from the mouth can ensnare the soul. Words from others can be a snare to the soul.

> A fool's mouth is his destruction, and his lips are the snare of his soul
>
> **Proverbs 18:7 (NKJV)**

By words, many have laid down their souls to the enemy. Satanic agents commonly use the channel of words, mostly through the tongue to ensnare the souls of many. There was a lady who jokingly said to another; "you like food so well, or will you sell me your birthright like Esau sold his to Jacob". The friend was awakened by the Holy Spirit and she screamed "No, I will not sell you my birthright". Many soul hunters target victims by playing around words a lot. They could say "you are so unfortunate", making it appear as a joke. Believers need to rise up and refute those words in Jesus' name, without being afraid they will be called "weird". Words are a common tool used to assess the soul of many. Some soul hunters use flattery to assess the soul of their victims as the Scripture notes:

> To deliver you from the immoral woman, From the seductress *who* flatters with her words, Who forsakes the companion of her youth, And forgets the covenant of her God. For her house leads down to death, And her paths to the dead; None who go to her return,Nor do they regain the paths of life—
> **Proverbs 2:16-19 (NKJV)**

The soul can become open to the devil through demonic praises, by participating in the wrong conversations, or by innocently agreeing to a satanic cause. Satanic agents are highly trained specialists in using words to capture souls. It is important that God's children watch what they say and agree with.

Spiritual Wars Against the Soul : Satanic Media and Contents or Books

Polluted media, written words motivated by the devil, or the wrong media contents - all these are deadly to godly souls. We stopped by a location of one of America's major bookstores. We were looking to purchase a copy of the Bible. To our surprise, right in front of the aisle where Bibles were shelved, there were also books for learning witchcraft practices. Immediately we were reminded of a young lady who informed us that she learned the recipe for rituals and witchcraft activities through the books her grandfather passed to her. There are books that believers should not be reading.

Around 2017, a young lady ran mad and began to take off her clothes during a church service. Someone who had been part of our Prophetic Worship Encounters at Lighthill recommended they take her to Lighthill Church. It was too late because she was already at the psychiatric hospital. They still called us for prayers. After praying, God said she was going to be released from the hospital by Monday. They had called on a Friday. We were wondering what really happened and why. God said this was an arrow fired from Africa which located the wrong individual. The Holy Spirit said the arrow located her because of a portal that the enemy had opened into her soul through demonic media. We asked her mother, and they brought out her phone and said she had been researching witchcraft and all sorts of satanist organizations and practices.

It is important for believers to shield their souls from all influences from satanic media.

PRAYERS TO WADE OFF THE WARS AGAINST THE SOUL

1. Lord Jesus, deliver my soul from the market of darkness in the name of Jesus.
2. My soul is set free from the cage of the enemy in the name of Jesus.
3. My soul is purged from the death that entered through satanic music, evil media and materials, in the name of Jesus.
4. My soul is delivered from pollution that entered through the wrong use of words, in the name of Jesus.
5. My soul is purged from the pollution that entered through unholy alliances, by the blood of Jesus.
6. My soul is purged from the pollution that entered into you through places of pollution, in the name of Jesus.
7. My soul is purged of any satanic food in the name of Jesus.
8. My soul shall be stable and steady in the name of Jesus
9. My soul is set free from all types of infirmity in the name of Jesus.
10. My soul is set free from the yoke of unholy sexual bondage in the name of Jesus.
11. My soul shall receive the power Word of God, in the name of Jesus.

JOURNAL

8

~

HEALED

SOUL

This chapter addresses the 3-process of rededication, deliverance, and healing of the soul for you to possess your soul and to be restored back to God. Jesus said, in Luke 21:19 - By your patience possesses your souls. In previous chapters, we learned that souls are very costly, and only the blood of Jesus satisfies its purchase requirement. Also, God has given us one of the revelations into why the soul is very costly, and we share that using a term we call - *The ToolBox of Destiny*. This revelation helps you understand why a lost soul, wounded soul, or imprisoned soul needs to go through the three-step process of rededication, deliverance, and healing.

At creation, every soul receives a name, purpose, and the tools for the purpose. All information needed by the soul on earth including the rules of life, gifts, and wisdom needed to fulfill that destiny is programmed into the soul and sealed up in what we call "The ToolBox of Destiny".

"Before I formed you in the womb I knew you; Before you were born I sanctified you; I ordained you a prophet to the nations."
Jeremiah 1:5 (NKJV)

The ToolBox of Destiny

This ToolBox of Destiny is the portfolio containing all master plans, files, and important information about each soul coming to the world. Every soul has a unique ToolBox of Destiny containing unique information implanted into that soul by the Lord. . The Lord writes a library of instructions about the lifetime of a soul at creation, makes a covenant with the soul, and keeps a copy of the document in His book, and the other copy is hidden in the newly created soul. This means every assignment given by God, and thought comes from our soul and is translated through the mind for our human understanding. It is already in us - the raw gifts, the idea of what we want to do in life. The raw gifts only need to be developed as we grow, because as a baby, the body cannot do much until it matures. The ToolBox of Destiny contains information pieces like the name of a child to be called on earth, rules governing the child's life, and other vital pieces that are highly impactful to the child. This includes the name they are to be called, just like it was said concerning Jesus before His birth:

> " For unto us a child is born, unto us a son is given, and the government will be on his shoulders. And he will be called Wonderful Counselor, Mighty God, Everlasting Father, Prince of Peace"
> **Isaiah 9:6 (NKJV)**

And similarly, just as the father of Samson asked the angel who came visiting about the destiny of Samson as stated in the Scriptures below:

> "Manoah said, "Now let Your words come *to pass!* What will be the boy's rule of life, and his work?"
> **Judges 13:12 (NKJV)**

Some parents, like the parents of Samson, and the parents of Jesus got this revelation, and as a result, they asked specific questions about their unborn child. It is recommended that parents take time to ask the Lord in their prayer time, especially the pregnant ones. "Lord, what is the name you have given this child"? "What defines this child's life? "What's the rule of the life of this child? And the Lord's answers will answer these prayers of inquiry.

Also in the Scripture below, Isaiah revealed that he was given a name while he was still in the womb.

Listen to me, O islands, and pay attention, O distant
peoples: The LORD called me from the womb; from the body
of my mother He named me.
Isaiah 49:1 (NKJV)

From these Scriptures above, we see how the portfolio of a
person's life has existed before they were born.

The Enemy's Plan to Compromise the Soul

God has secured the ToolBox of Destiny such that satan is unable
to steal the information therein. However, he is able to access that
information if given a chance and sets up distractions to waste
lives to hinder destiny's fulfillment. Also, satan can steal souls,
though he is unable to use the ToolBox of Destiny in the soul for
anything good.

Satanic agents do observe the purpose of souls. Some
souls are ordained as Builders, Helpers, Teachers, Pioneers, and
some Crafters. They are able to analyze a general overview of a
person's life assignment, and they use different tactics to corrupt
the soul knowing that a corrupt soul loses access to God's
presence. When access is lost to God's presence, there is no way to
unlock the ToolBox of Destiny containing the important pieces
for direction into destiny. This is why people's souls are a high
target for the enemy and the major reason for polluting souls is
to ruin God's assignment over their lives. When a soul is polluted,
a soul becomes sick and no longer stands in God's presence. Also,
when the enemy steals souls, he tramples upon the soul, locks the

soul up in the prison of darkness and wastes the entire purpose of a soul.

3 Layers of Warfare Against the Soul

The enemy fights the soul with three types of war. The Scripture reminds us in John 10:10 "The thief does not come except to steal, and to kill, and to destroy...". The words "Steal", "Kill" and "Destroys" represent the 3 layers of warfare of the enemy against the soul. If the soul no defense in wartime the following can occur

1. **Wounding of the Soul:** A wounded soul is a soul that is injured. The soul is no longer in a healthy state and the goal of the enemy is to snuff out the life of the soul. Psalm 56:13 stated, "For You have delivered my soul from death. *Have You* not *kept* my feet from falling, That I may walk before God.In the light of the living?" All types of emotional pains and affliction originate from a wounded soul. It is mostly caused when the soul is exposed to disappointments and heartbreaks. Symptoms of a wounded soul include difficulty in forgiving and anger. This can affect the soul's relationship with the Lord. This is usually found in some believers who have experienced hurt but finding it hard to let go, or having marital problems or emotional issues. The enemy usually fires such wounds to disrupt a soul's unity with God and steal peace away from the soul to cause distraction. If left unresolved, it could lead to the imprisonment of the soul, or losing the soul to the devil.

2. **Imprisonment of the Soul:** An imprisoned soul has been locked up in the cage of the enemy to prevent the soul from fulfilling its purpose. Psalm 124:7 speaks about the Psalmist's soul rejoicing after escape from the prison - "Our soul has escaped as a bird from the snare of the fowlers; The snare is broken, and we have escaped". A soul can be imprisoned, when this happens, the person's mind is locked with satanic chains. Symptoms of an imprisoned soul are extreme laziness, wasteful living, joblessness, inability to become productive, anger, addiction, abusiveness, cheating spouses, lying, and much more. This is usually the case for many drunkards, spouses who are cheating, and people who are usually lazy and nothing seems to work for them. Some people whose souls are in captivity genuinely desire repentance, and hope for it but lack the power to enter into it. This is a symptom of a soul held captive by the devil.

3. **Lost Soul:** A lost soul has been stolen by the enemy. The Scripture notes in Mark 8:36 about the risk of losing the soul "For what shall it profit a man if he shall gain the whole world, and lose his own soul?". A soul has been lost when the soul becomes indifferent to the ways of God. Many souls are currently lost, as the enemy has brought them into a place of complacency concerning the worship of the Living God. A lost soul is described in detail in 1 Timothy 4: 1-2 - "Now the Spirit expressly says that in latter times some will depart from the faith, giving heed to deceiving spirits and doctrines of demons, speaking lies in hypocrisy, having their own conscience

seared with a hot iron". Symptoms are: the heart is no longer a heart filled with the love and compassion of God, the heart becomes the heart of stone, and there is no remorse when caught in sin. Sinful living is a part of life. Such souls avoid the Word of God or the truth that sets them free. This is mostly found in people who will never accept Jesus and people who are working in the spirit of darkness such as divination, witchcraft, mediums, and related occults. One major identifier of a lost soul is that they have accepted the defeat of hell and are never touched by the news of the second coming, the upcoming judgment of the Lord Jesus. One of the last provisions made for such souls is for them to be won by the mercies of the Lord.

Dedication of the Soul

A soul must first be rededicated back to the Lord Jesus before the journey into healing. Say the prayers below loud to dedicate your soul back to the Lord.

PRAYER OF DEDICATION OF THE SOUL

Father, I give my soul back to you, I acknowledge that you created my soul and ordained me for a great purpose, and you sent your Son Jesus, the Savior to die for my sins and the Author of Life to give me a beautiful destiny in your will. Let the blood of Jesus speak for me and redeem my soul for your glory, in Jesus' Name.

Amen

Deliverance of the Soul and Mind

Now that you have dedicated your soul back to the Lord. The next step is to walk in God's deliverance from all the traumatic encounters.

"But thus says the Lord: "Even the captives of the mighty shall be taken away, And the prey of the terrible be delivered; For I will contend with him who contends with you, And I will save your children".
Isaiah 49:25 (NKJV)

Deliverance begins by knowing that you are separated from the past. The mind must no longer allow any form of darkness into the soul. When the mind is free of all forms of sin such as idol worship, lust, and drunkenness, and focused on the ways of Jesus, the Lord becomes the Deliverer and commands captivity to end. In deliverance, the blood of Jesus fights for the souls and restores the soul back to the Lord. This is why Ezekiel 18:4 noted, "Behold, all souls are mine; as the soul of the father, so also the soul of the son is mine: the soul that sinneth, it shall die". Only the Lord's hand can put a stop to any war that the enemy rages against the soul. The Lord owns all souls, the ones He redeems, He snatches out of the devil's hands, and the one He condemns, he hands over to the devil. The deliverance of the soul ensures the activities of demons are put to a stop by casting them out and putting an end to sinful desires.

Healing of the Soul

At this stage, the soul is seeking healing in order to become prosperous. The Scripture points out a very important prayer which is the basis of the healing of the soul in 3 John 1:2, "Beloved, I pray that you may prosper in all things and be in health, just as your soul prospers". Prosperity of the soul is a condition of the soul that the healing of the soul brings. Other Scriptures also inform about different conditions of the soul. Some souls are in a hungry state, some in a sorrowful state, weary, sick, bitter, and some souls are joyful. Also, the book of 3 John 1:2 also further expands on the prosperity of the soul. A prosperous soul advances in the will and in the ways of God. King David went through healing of the soul and said in Psalm 23:3, "restore my soul. He leads me in the path of righteousness". When a soul is undergoing the healing process, it learns about righteous living, so it does not fall back into the past ways of life. As a general rule, when a soul is restored and delivered, righteous living follows for completeness and maintenance of healing.

Let Your Soul Trust and Worship God Only: Every soul going through healing must always commit their soul into God's hands and trust only in God. You should not commit or outsource your mind and soul to others because human beings are not perfect. The Lord warned in the book of Jeremiah 17:5, "Cursed is the man who trusts in mankind And makes flesh his strength, And whose heart turns away from the LORD". For this reason, it is always safe to make the Lord our trust and source. Trusting in the Lord draws us to worship the Lord only.

Feed on the Word of God: The Word of God teaches, in James 1:21 - "Therefore lay aside all filthiness and overflow of wickedness, and receive with meekness the implanted word, which is able to save your souls". God's Word is needed for the stability of the soul. A believer must grow every moment in God's Word and can do so by reading, studying, and meditating. The soul must also be guarded by the Word of God and the power of the Holy Spirit.

Finally, the only sure way to possess and connect your soul to the Lord is by emulating Jesus. When you emulate Jesus, the Kingdom of God becomes your focus and your soul no longer desires the worldly ways that war against your soul.

PRAYERS FOR THE HEALING OF THE SOUL

1. My soul belongs to the Lord Jesus.
2. I dedicate my soul back to the Lord, in the name of Jesus.
3. Father, deliver my soul from the hands of wickedness in the name of Jesus.
4. Father, deliver my soul from the captivity of darkness in the name of Jesus.
5. Father, deliver my soul from the power of the grave in the name of Jesus
6. My Father, guard my mind by the fire of the Holy Spirit in the name of Jesus
7. My soul, hear the Word of the Lord, you shall not yield to darkness in the name of Jesus
8. Angels of the Lord, be on guard to watch over my soul in the name of Jesus
9. My soul is not for sale because the blood of Jesus has purchased my soul in the name of Jesus.
10. All traps of the wicked shall not catch my soul, but shall catch the soul of the wicked in the name of Jesus
11. All clutter in my soul blocking the revelation of Jesus Christ is purged out by the fire of the Holy Spirit.
12. My soul is restored into God's original state for the fulfillment of purpose in the name of Jesus.
13. The powers of the emptiers and wasters of the soul are

destroyed in the name of Jesus.

14. My soul shall not be wounded in the name of Jesus.

15. My soul will not be wasted in the name of Jesus.

16. Every cloud of darkness over my mind is consumed by the power of the Holy Ghost in the name of Jesus.

17. Every vomit of darkness is flushed out of my soul by the purifying fire of the Holy Spirit, in the name of Jesus

18. All deposits of filthiness in my soul are flushed out by the purifying fire of the Holy Spirit, in the name of Jesus

19. My soul receives deep cleansing, in the name of Jesus.

20. No longer will my soul be out of connection to God's Spirit, in the name of Jesus.

21. Let the original covenant written on the day my soul was created be restored unto my soul in the name of Jesus.

22. Father, uphold my soul to continue in your worship in the name of Jesus.

PROPHETIC WORD RELEASE

Need to Receive Prophetic or Deliverance Ministry Online ?

SCHEDULE A TIME

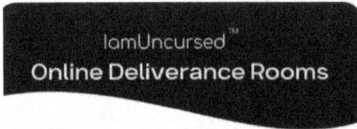

ZOOM
8PM to 9PM EST
Mondays

IamUncursed™
Online Deliverance Rooms

Online Deliverance, Prayer and Prophecy Rooms

- Deliverance Bible Study
- Deliverance Prayers Rooms
- Prophecy Rooms

www.iamuncursed.com

Email: Hello@iamuncursed.com to schedule a FREE prophecy room appointment

LOOKING TO PURSUE YOUR DELIVERANCE OR PROPHETIC OR PROPHETIC WORSHIP MINISTRY CALLING?

Enroll at the IAUC Online School of Ministry to begin or advance your Deliverance, Prophetic and Prophetic Ministry calling through our Online Ministry Programs:

Email the IAUC Program Team:
hello@iamuncursed.com

Deliverance for the Deliverance Ministers Join the Largest Deliverance Ministers' Platform

Getting Married?
Or Seeking Marriage Restoration?

Read the Heaven's Gateway to a Blissful Marriage
Book and Workbook
Enroll in the Marriage Preparation or Marriage
deliverance course:
hello@blissfulmarriageuniversity.com

Blissful Marriage University

MARRIAGE READINESS
AND
DELIVERANCE COURSE

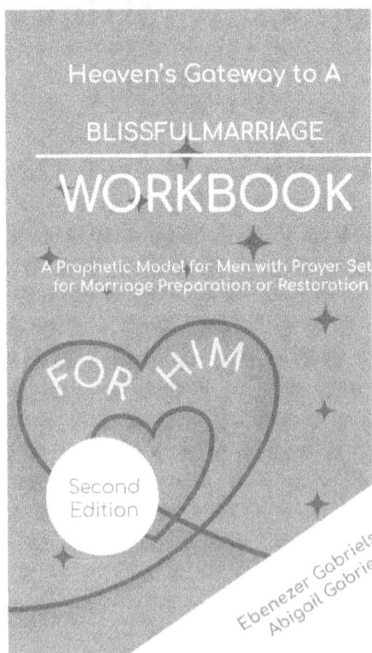

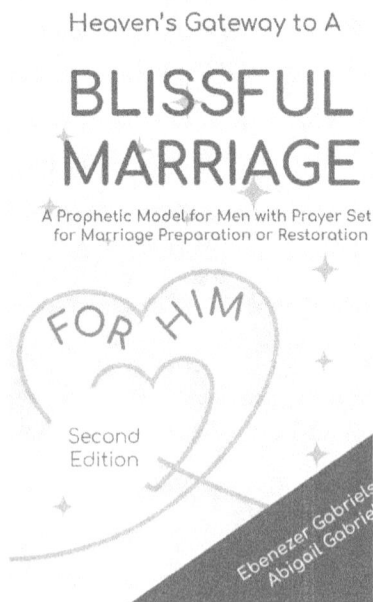

ABOUT THE I AM UNCURSED ONLINE COMMUNITY

A Biblical Deliverance, Deliverance Education, and Curse-Breaking Platform

The deliverance of Jesus is here. Uncursed has grown from a stack of prayer pages carried around in a folder, to the Uncursed book available in multi-languages and to the I am Uncursed community, a deliverance, and curse-breaking platform. At iamuncursed.com, we are sharing God's Word of deliverance and of power in dynamic ways; through deliverance devotionals, expiration of on-demand deliverance topics, and most importantly, Bible study on deliverance. Uncursed is the platform for deliverance discipleship. Ministers of deliverance and seekers of deliverance are getting delivered now, and being equipped for the next season in their lives.

The deliverance ministry is needed across; there are only a few vessels that have obtained the authority to minister deliverance. God is planting His Word into the souls of His people, so that they may learn deliverance from His Word and through the teachings of anointed leaders. I am Uncursed is the destination for deliverance discipleship including learning about deliverance for personal growth or ministry growth, exploring deliverance topics, shop deliverance resources, and growing in the deep spiritual knowledge of Jesus.

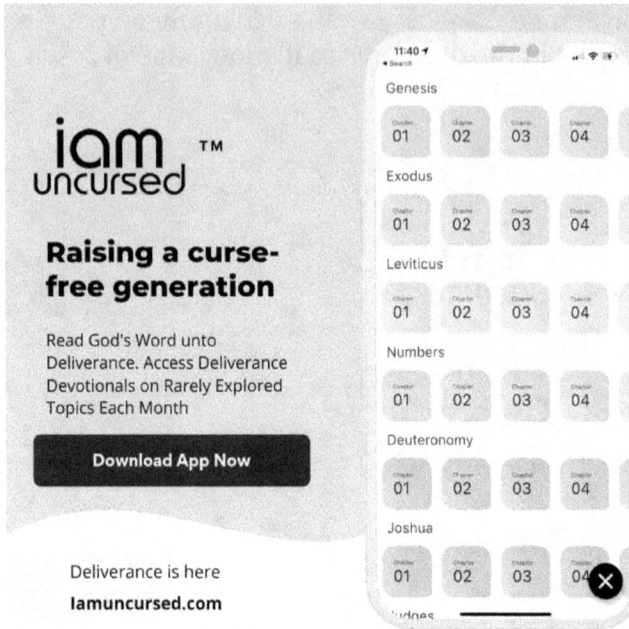

ABOUT THE AUTHORS

About the Authors

Ebenezer Gabriels is a Worshiper, Innovation Leader, Prophetic Intercessor, and a Computer Scientist who has brought heaven's solutions into Financial markets, Technology, and Government with his computational gifts. Prophet Gabriels is anointed as a Prophetic Leader of nations with the mantle of healing, worship music, national deliverance, foundational deliverance, complex problem-solving, and building Yahweh's worship altars.

Abigail Ebenezer-Gabriels is Pastor, Teacher, Worshiper, and

Multi-disciplinary leader in Business, Technology, Education, and Development. She is blessed with prophetic teaching abilities with the anointing to unveil the mysteries in the Word of God. She is a Multi-specialty Speaker, with a special anointing to explain Heaven's ordinances on earth.

Both Ebenezer Gabriels and Abigail Ebenezer-Gabriels are the founders of the Ebenezer Gabriels Schools Leadership Education comprising 5 leadership schools including *I am Uncursed for* MINISTRY, *Blissful Marriage University for* SINGLES AND MARRIED, *Unprofaned Purpose for* BUSINESS, *InspireMyLittleOne* for YOUNG INNOVATORS and iThinkicode for Engineers.

They are church planters and Senior Pastors of LightHill Church, Flames of Worship, and lead several worship communities including the 6-Hour Worship unto Deliverance, Innovation Lab Worship encounters, Move this Cloud - and prophetic podcast communities including the Daily Prophetic Insights and Prophetic Fire where God's agenda for each day is announced and the manifold wisdom of God is revealed on earth. Both Ebenezer Gabriels and his wife, Abigail Ebenezer-Gabriels joyfully serve the Lord through lifestyles of worship and their mandate is to build worship altars to intercede for nations.

**Ebenezer
Gabriels**
ministries

About Ebenezer Gabriels

At Ebenezer Gabriels Ministries (EGM), we fulfill the mandate of building worship altars by sharing the story of the most expensive worship ever offered by Jesus Christ, the Son of God and dispersing the aroma of the knowledge of Jesus Christ to the ends of the world.

Explore the Ebenezer Gabriels Communities

Deliverance: www.iAmuncursed.com
Singles: compass.blissfulmarriageuniversity.com
Marriage: www.Blissfulmarriageuniversity.com
Children's: www.inspiremylittleone.com
Business: www.unprofanedpurpose.com
Prophetic Worship Evangelistic Discipleship Missions: www.ebenezergabriels.org

Ebenezer Gabriels Publishing delivers biblically grounded learning experiences that prepare audiences for launch into their prophetic calling. We create educational content and deliver in innovative ways through online classrooms, apps, audio, and prints to enhance the experience of each audience as they are filled with the aroma of Christ knowledge and thrive in their worship journey.

EGM currently operates out of Gaithersburg in Maryland, USA.

CONTACT

Mailing
19644 Club House Road Suite 815, Gaithersburg, Maryland,
20876 USA

iamuncursed.com
hello@ebenezergabriels.org
www.ebenezergabriels.org

Other Books in the Uncursed Series

UNCURSED SERIES

The
Prophetic &
Spiritually
Intelligent
MOTHER

Featuring

Angelic Execution of
Contracts of Your Child's Life

Important Spiritual Dates

Spiritual Encounters of Children

Your Child's Dominant Anointing

The Spiritual Territory of Your Child

The Name of a Child

The Prophetic Mother's Prayers

Ebenezer Gabriels
Abigail Gabriels

Other Books by Ebenezer and Abigail Gabriels

Worship

Worship is Expensive

War of Altars

Business and Purpose

Unprofaned Purpose for Business

Elements of Time

Spirit of Teams

Kids

Activating my Prophetic Senses for Kids

Bree Learns about Processes

Places we went - Jerusalem

The Excellent Spirit of Daniel

The Birth of a King

Places we went - Uganda

Marriage

Heaven's Gate way to a Blissful marriage for Him

Heaven's Gateway to a Blissful marriage for Her

Deliverance from the Yokes of Marital Ignorance

Pulling Down the Strongholds of Evil Participants in Marriage

Prophetic

The Prophetic System

Activating Your Prophetic Senses

Dreams and Divine Interpretations

Relationships (singles)

Heaven's Compass for Cultivating a Blissful Pre-Marital Atmosphere for Her

Heaven's Compass for Cultivating a Blissful Pre-Marital Atmosphere for Him

Deliverance

Uncursed

Deliverance from the Yoke of Accursed Names

Deliverance from the Curse of Vashti

Deliverance from the Yoke of Incest

Deliverance from the Wrong Family Tree

Principles of Prophetic Deliverance

Mind

Deliverance from the Yokes Deep Mysteries of Creation in the Realms of Thoughts, Imaginations and Words

Spiritual War and Prayers

Blazing Sword of the Lord

Rapid Fire

The Big Process called Yoke

Deliverance of the Snares of the Fowler

The only Fire that Extinguishes Witchcraft

No longer Fugitives of the Earth

Subduers of the Earth

Prayers of the Decade

Manifold Mysteries of Water

Growth and Advancing in Faith

Men: Called out of the Dunghill

Women: Bearers of Faith

New Beginnings in Christ

Wisdom my Companion

Deeper Mysteries of the Blood

Nations and intercessions

The Scroll and the Seal

America: The Past, the Present and the Next Chapter

Herod: The Church and Nigeria

Prophetic Insights into the Year

21 Weapons of Survival for 2021

2022 Meet the God Who Saves Blesses Shepherds and Carries

Soul

Deeper Mysteries of the Soul (English, Spanish, Arabic and

Chinese)

Unmute my Soul

Uncursed Series

The Spiritually Intelligent Mother

Ebenezer-Gabriels Digital Communities

Explore the Ebenezer Gabriels Platforms

Spiritual War and Deliverance: www.IAmUncursed.com

Marriage: www.Blissfulmarriageuniversity.com

Children's: www.inspiremylittleone.com

Business and Marketplace: www.unprofanedpurpose.com

Ebenezer Gabriels Schools of the Holy Spirit and On Demand TV : www.ebenezergabriels.org

www.ingramcontent.com/pod-product-compliance
Lightning Source LLC
LaVergne TN
LVHW051813080426
835513LV00017B/1937